SUSTAIN YOURSELF ORACLE

A Handbook & Cards for Using Earth's Wisdom for Personal Transformation

James Wanless, Ph.D.

FAIR WINDS

Inspiring | Educating | Creating | Entertaining

Brimming with creative inspiration, how-to projects, and useful information to enrich your everyday life, quarto.com is a favorite destination for those pursuing their interests and passions.

This edition published in 2023.
First edition published in 2011 by Fair Winds Press, an imprint of The Quarto Group,
100 Cummings Center, Suite 265-D, Beverly, MA 01915, USA.
T (978) 282-9590 F (978) 283-2742 Quarto.com

Fair Winds Press titles are also available at discount for retail, wholesale, promotional, and bulk purchase. For details, contact the Special Sales Manager by email at specialsales@quarto.com or by mail at The Quarto Group, Attn: Special Sales Manager, 100 Cummings Center, Suite 265-D, Beverly, MA 01915, USA.

27 26 25 24 23   1 2 3 4 5

ISBN: 978-0-7603-8172-4

Originally published by Tarot Media Company, a Cigno E Gallo, Inc. Company
San Francisco, California
www.TarotMediaCompany.com

Design and Page Layout: Maggie Cote
Cover Images: Cards by James Wanless, background textures by Olivia Hutcherson and Tim Mossholder on Unsplash. Blue feather image by Daniel Olah on Unsplash.
Interior Background Images: Shutterstock

Printed in China

The information in this book is for educational purposes only. It is not intended to replace the advice of a physician or medical practitioner. Please see your health-care provider before beginning any new health program.

Inspired by the Earth's wisdom, this book and set of cards are dedicated to sustaining life on Earth.

CONTENTS

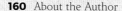

Part One

SUSTAINABLE LIFE

1. The Sustain Ability Imperative

Sustainability has become a dominant life value and guiding principle for the modern world because it is more than necessary, it is imperative. To ensure our futures and our very survival as a species, sustainability is an ability that we must cultivate as a way of life.

Sustainable life means living well and living long. To do this requires living whole — which means to stay healthy, be happy, grow wise, have sufficient material wealth, be creative, adaptable and resilient, preserve the earth, contribute to community and social harmony — all in a conscious and balanced way.

Because of the totally interconnected and interdependent nature of modern life along with the technology revolution and a bursting worldwide population that demands copious energy and material goods, we now have the capability of completely destroying ourselves and our biospheric home through the proliferation of nuclear arms and by depleting and polluting the natural environment that supports life.

Moreover, personal sustainability — living an enduring quality-of-life — has become uppermost in our lives because of the mushrooming demands and volatile conditions of the 21st century.

We are confronted with increasing amounts and speed of change as never before. Even change is changing.

We are overwhelmed with exponentially increasing information, sheer volume of numbers in terms of population and everything else — all leading to incomprehensible complexities.

We are conflicted over growing diversity, social fragmentation, political conflict, and economic inequalities.

We are confronted with mind boggling choices and possibilities that paralyze us.

We face robust and relentless competition.

We experience technological advances ahead of the ability of our cultures, mindsets, and even our DNA to integrate into our way of being.

We are plagued by modern day diseases and psychological-emotional pathologies that did not exist before.

We feel lost as we are enveloped within a fragile bubble of stressful and exhausting uncertainty, setbacks, crises, and unforeseen and unintended consequences of monumental proportions.

The sum of these circumstances has presented us with unprecedented challenges for which we have no clear means of managing successfully.

To this dangerous and daunting mix of tests and trials, our expectations for the quality of life we want has risen and risen. We desire more and demand better. It's not enough to just get by, we want it all. As our standards get higher, the ability to sustain becomes more critical — and more difficult. When we have more to lose, our drive to preserve and maintain what we have intensifies.

Dramatic increases in our length of life have made sustainability an inexorable, overriding theme of our existence. We are inescapably forced to again and again meet the exigencies of the 21st century. The "holy grail" of our lives today is the sustain ability to "Re"-Re-charge, Re-store, Re-start, Re-new.

The length, demands and changes of life require that we continually "re" ourselves — re-energize our bodies, recharge emotionally, reinvent work, rekindle relationships, re-stimulate our mind, rethink everything, recover from misfortunes, rebalance life, redis-cover ourselves, rebuild communities, restore environment, and revive our spirits.

2. The New Sustain Abilities

EVOLUTIONARY AWARENESS

Every living organism and society has always focused on sustainability, but to endure and recycle ourselves through these wild times of transformation and risk requires nothing less than an evolutionary life style. The sustain-able life is an evolved way of living.

The skills of sustainability — "sustain abilities" — are, in fact, evolutionary traits that can carry us through times of personal and global change.

What's new and different about the sustain abilities in the modern world is the aware-ness that we are evolving at this very moment in consciousness, in behavior, and in body. The new emergent scientific field of epigenetics indicates that our culture and lifestyle are creating transformations within us that impact our cellular memory, all resulting in new know-how. The world and ourselves are speeding up, and so we are called upon to keep up to sustain.

Commitment to an evolving life means that we intentionally grow ourselves and fulfill all our human potentials. Personal and social growth is the core driving force that sustains us through challenging times — not who we have been, not outdated ways that once worked, either of which are even remotely suitable to the new ways of the world.

EXPONENTIAL CREATIVITY

An evolving, growth-oriented life must be constantly creative and adaptive as never before in human history. It is by our own cherished values of creativity and innovation that we have generated this 21st century radical unfoldment. The more we create, the more we must cre-ate to keep up. To sustain in an exponentially changing world, we must create, create, create. It's a bit like chasing our own tail, but chase we must.

WHOLE-INTERDEPENDENT-ONE

Though some elements of personal sustainability are as they have always been, like moving your body to stay physically healthy, it's when we look at ourselves as an interconnected energy field, we see how body and mind; inner self and outer world of people, work, environment; and consciousness and technology are absolutely interdependent. These need to be sustained by synchronized and compatible means. This requires a comprehensive, wholistic view of sustainability calling for a kind of new "Declaration of Interdependence."

We are experiencing surprising and sometimes dismaying crossover impacts and conse-quences of the wholeness factor.

For example, we now know that friendships are as vital to physical longevity as diet and exercise. Studies have concurred that happiness and obesity are contagious, so in a way, we are our friends. If we spend time with happy people, we tend to be happier; if we spend time with people who overeat and don't exercise, we find ourselves overconsuming and experiencing "sedentary behavior disorder."

We understand today how energy-depleting and dehumanizing our way of working is. Work as we have known it in the past does not work for today because we have changed. No longer a place of dignity, service and excellence, the workplace is now focused on the singular profit motive and so instead of creative satisfaction and spiritual fulfillment, work has become the source of heart attacks, mind-numbing inertia, physical fatigue, and emotional stress and anxiety. Instead of creating and preserving life, work can kill.

Sustainability needs to be holistically reformulated and created anew as we re-vision ourselves, our beliefs, and our stories of how to live, and as we re-form our social mores and institutions to fit our changing selves.

Amidst the new rules of sustainability, the ancient and venerable law of oneness, the coherence theory of truth — "as above, so below" — is essential to know today. This yesteryear adage and universal truth — there being no separation between outside events in our lives and how we are within us — must be remembered, respected and revitalized. So, an energy crisis in the world is mirrored by our own personal energy crisis. Pollution of the environment is reflected in our own toxic food and drinks. Stormy international relations echo our interpersonal relationships and our own internal conflicts. The sustain ability is to sustain yourself, others and the world simultaneously for all are inherently connected.

In accordance with this renewed perspective of oneness, the new sustain abilities are the very same evolved qualities of life that we look forward to having. The means and the ends are identical. Happiness is a sustain ability and we want to be happy, so be happy and bring a smile to others. To live healthfully is a sustain ability and we all desire to be healthy, so live healthy and ensure that the soil from which you eat is healthy. Material success is a sustain ability, so get your finances together, and at the same time empower others to succeed to create a world of true prosperity. A sustain-able life occurs under conditions of peace, therefore live in harmony with yourself and be cooperative with each other and with nature.

BE THE CHANGE

Given the interdependent nature of life, "Be the change you want to see in the world" is a foremost sustain ability on this changing planet. Personal responsibility is social responsibility, and vice versa. It's a genuinely healthy selfish thing to protect the health and peace of our social and natural environments, but narrow self-centeredness unconnected to the collective, which breeds social apathy, cynicism, negligence, greed, hypocrisy and blame are unsustainable traits. The sustain abilities must be as directed to the wellness of our own personal self-ecology as to the outside world as one living being.

SECURITY FROM WITHIN

A sustainable world results under conditions of safety and security, and so we must, like all creatures and organisms, be able to defend ourselves and feel protected. The best safeguard and deterrent in our evolving human world is having a sense of self-confidence and self-sufficiency.

Act like atoms, which are the most basic elements from which we are made. Thus, our "atomic life" is about interacting but not interposing in another's affairs, as exemplified by how atoms actually do coexist. Atom bombs and armies are a fundamentally maladaptive strategy for being safe. Weapons in our interdependent world, like the misuse of how atoms naturally exist, breed suspicion and fear, and lead to war and unsustainable life.

COMPETITION

Naturally, there is competition at every level of life. It takes an evolved way of looking at competition to realize that instead of an unsustainable dog-eat-dog mentality (that, in fact, does not exist for the most part in nature), competing is a win-win way of coexisting and collaborating. Competitors are meant to be noble adversaries who challenge us to bring out the best in ourselves as they act from their own best selves. Competition that does not destroy and denigrate is a sustain ability and evolutionary force to be embraced.

RENEWABLE SYNERGY

Sustainability demands physical energy and we all want to be energetic and have an active life for a long time. To do this, tap the renewable sources of energy within you and around you into a synergistic powerhouse, which is comparable to the way the sun, our power source of life, re-energizes itself. (The origin of synergy is "sun ergos" which means "working together.") Without a synergistic combination of the diverse energies within ourselves and those that compose our world and natural planet, we have "unergy," an exponential decrease of power.

SYNERGIZE AND RE-ENERGIZE YOURSELF BY:

Teaming together your "inner selves" such as your inner guard for self-protection, your inner doctor to heal yourself, your inner mover and shaker to keep you going, your inner captain to navigate life, your inner magician to manifest visions and dreams, your inner wise woman to know.

Activating the subtle energy centers (often referred to as chakras) for powering up your heart of emotions and their expression; your intuitive mind of clarity and genius; your base physical drives and desires; and your connection to the higher power as your greatest ally.

Plugging into the zeitgeist or prevailing collective energy of the times and the vitality of a place and people.

Feeding on the super food of the natural elements — pure sunlight, oxygen, water, and the organic bounty of earth.

Seeking out stimulating diversity within yourself (your different personas) and in the world of diverse cultures, races, ethnic groups and ways of life.

Avoiding energy-depleting thoughts, negative situations, unhealthy relationships, and toxic environments.

EMOTION INTO MOTION!

Sustainable living is joyous and motivated, otherwise, who cares? We want to be turned on, be happy and have fun. In a way, fun is the new fun-damentalism of the sustainability path — play is precious, laughter is healing, happiness is contagious, love is superglue, joy is magic, enthusiasm is success, ecstasy is creative, bliss is divine.

Trusting our emotions, following and expressing them in constructive ways keeps our heart ticking. Our very life force is pulsed and embodied by passion. Emotions set us in motion and keep us in motion. All emotions motivate and transform us. Anger can move us to power and righteous indignation; sorrow to releasing and clearing away the old; stagnation to germination; fear to healthy concern and protection.

If we are not moved by feelings to move, we are rigor mortis, dead.

INTUITIVE THINKING

While sustainable life is fueled by feelings, it is governed by wisdom. Smart decisions in today's changing, shifting, growing world cannot be had by old thinking of obsolete beliefs and languaging, and over-reliance on linear left brain logic — all of which are enormously energy-consuming, slow, ineffective, and polluted by negative thoughts.

Intuitive thinking brings us an up-to-date, swift and adaptable, savvy way of navigating life. This kind of "energy thinking" is founded upon the following essentials:

- information-gathering;
- mental equanimity;
- emotional equilibrium;
- imagination;
- integration and inventory of physical senses, life experience, present situations and personal authenticity in considering decisions;
- action on the impulse.

Think in a blink. But first, get the information, get centered, feel the feeling, trust it and act upon it. It's twenty-first century logic that works for a tired and confused brain overwhelmed by paralysis by analysis.

APOTHEOSIS — THE FUTURE PULL

Sustainability is attained by the spiritual understanding of life as the process of apotheosis — hearing the call of divine mission, our raison d'etre, and responding with all our being to achieve our highest spiritual destiny. We all want to be deeply fulfilled by living with purpose and meaning, which manifests through inspiration ("in-spirited"). Led by this inexorable pull of spirit — our life force — we are pulled by the future as destiny beckons. Life becomes easier, and in a more relaxed way, we flow with the flow of spirited living.

AUTHENTICITY IS AUTHOR

Highly sustainable life is the creation of authentic individuals, those who follow their own feelings, intuition, impulses, and inspiration. Only when we are authentic can we embody and manifest our unique genius and fullest self-expression. By extolling the value of our own individuality, individuation, self-realization and self-actualization, we give ourselves the best chance for optimum living by authoring our lives our own way.

Subconsciously, we all follow roles that have been scripted for us by others. The day we wake up is when we discover that we have been living someone else's story. By choosing an authentic way of being, we author our own life journey. In making up our own story, we create a life of integrity and certainty. With an inner core of resoluteness and truth, this rock-solid life withstands the vicissitudes, the downturns, and the unpredictability of our changing world, which so often takes us off course and dissolves our will and aspiration.

RIGHT LIVELIHOOD WORKS

As always, sustained living requires being productive for gaining basic sustenance. We like to work, be successful, and have material prosperity. The traditional success ethic still thrives, though sustainability is the new success. True and lasting sustainable productivity can only truly be attained by following the principles of right livelihood, in which our work is our life path and purpose, our practiced and practical skill set, our passion and play, and our profession and profits. Work is meant to be love made visible and shared. Spread the love, do your authentic work and then you can work and work and work. It's not about retirement, it's refirement! Let your passion for your work set you on fire to achieve your personal highest good and make your contribution to the highest good for all.

BEFRIEND TO BELONG

As social animals, we want friends and need friends to sustain. Now that one quarter of the American public has nobody to talk to in a meaningful way, it is a society at risk. Communicate to communicate is the way to community. All media and mediums link us and all have significant value. Find your tribe, build your team, extend your family, connect online, volunteer, meet up, join a class, reach out, sign up and show up in the world are all ways to sustain our primordial need for belonging.

New and necessary relationship skills are honed through proactive practices — our Emotional Intelligence Quotient, or EQ, can — and must — be raised. Kindness toward others is the virtue most sought in a relationship partner. Empathy has become the indispensable social skill for connecting. Discernment is the new judgment. Compassion has made its way from spiritual traditions into mainstream culture. Doctors are now taught that the first rule of healing is to engage the patient, and only then, educate, enroll and prescribe. We cannot not communicate.

BALANCE RULES

None of these sustain abilities can be sustained unless life is led in balance. Since we strive to do it all and have it all, we must possess the balance to do this and that — to acquire and reduce, to expand and contract, to use and replace, to risk and restrain, to have more and less, to be mental and physical, to be introspective and extroverted, to serve oneself and others, to be independent and collaborative, to be material and spiritual, to consume and produce, to manage the highs and the lows, and, and, and... Live in the "and."

Balance is the core sustain ability for our hybrid and hyphenated existence of "both-and" rather than the either/or mentality that denies and divides. Our multi-cultural, multi-channel, multi-media, multi-dimensional, inter-disciplinary, inter-species, inter-denominational, cross-training, cross-marketing, cross-fertilization, co-mingling, co-evolving, co-creating world compels a balancing act.

SUSTAIN THE NOW BY SAVING FOR THE FUTURE

One of the most pressing balancing dances for being sustain-able is caring for the present and the future.

True sustainability only counts if our efforts sustain succeeding generations. Sustainability necessitates investing in the future, and we all want our children and their children to have a better life. This is really nothing new, except that in our current way of living, short-sighted focus on immediate gratification and momentary gains tend to dominate over far-sighted planning and restraint.

Realize, however, that by sacrificing in the now to create a better long-term future, we actually sustain and help ourselves in our present lifetime. If we prune back, for example, our consumption habits and spending to balance our financial accounts for the future, we fulfill our lives by engaging in other creative values and activities that are investments which grow ourselves and others into the fuller realization of all our potentials and sustain abilities.

To sacrifice is actually a redirection for redressing our out-of-balance behavior. Balance rules again, and always. And so, if we are holding off too much for the future, we may become unbalanced by not properly caring for the present. Life is truly a continual process of balancing, the ultimate sustain ability.

THINK HEALTHY EVERYTHING

All of these sustain abilities are for naught if we deplete and poison ourselves, our societies, and our natural environment. We must be ever-vigilant against toxic behavior so that we survive and thrive. Health is the new wealth in our whole way of life.

This means having a healthy environment, a healthy society, a healthy body, a healthy mind, a healthy outlook, a healthy heart, a healthy appetite, a healthy competition, a healthy business, a healthy family, a healthy relationship, a healthy future. Think health, and turn healthy thoughts to healthy actions, and everything will sustain.

REPEAT AND NOT DEPLETE

None of these sustain abilities are a one-time, one-off deal. They all require repetition, but we know that to repeat and repeat can deplete us. We want to be new and renewed in our youth-oriented culture, but how to generate and create ourselves anew? The secret for this most miraculous gift, often called the "fountain of youth," is found within our own human nature as nature. To apply within ourselves how nature cycles and recycles itself again and again is the solution. Nature can rescue and resuscitate us if we embody her ways. Live natural to live long and well.

Part Two

THE SUSTAINABILITY ROADMAP

3. Nature Knows

What is the way?
Lovely flowers open by the mossy roadside; The green willows dance in the spring breezes.
— Anonymous

The personal and collective roadmap for sustainability is nature. Nature knows how. Nature knows how to carry on through its sustain abilities, which are the essential capabilities that the Earth's biosphere has aplenty for creating an enduring and abundant life.

Nature has an astonishing genius for longevity, having sustained itself over billions of years. Nature's "green wisdom" knows how — how to create, change, grow and evolve so that it continually regenerates and renews. But nature, itself, has undergone several complete extinctions as have many civilizations, all showing the truth that we cannot be complacent and take for granted that everything will somehow turn out alright. Nature is never lazy, idle or indolent.

Nature knows energy, how to generate it, save it, not waste or pollute it. Our biosphere is the ultimate synergy of dynamic diversity. It is whole and self-creating, having the wisdom and power to replicate itself so that it sustains far into the future. Earth's ecology is the quintessential recycler, renewer, the "Re" expert.

Natural organisms know how to stay motivated and be fulfilled. In nature it's quite simple, for all organic life has an incessant and enthusiastic drive to live. Our task in life is to sustain this kind of wholehearted zest to "make a living," which in our world today is far more than just sheltering, feeding and reproducing ourselves. To make a living now means to sustain a living, and this includes all the joys, decisions, changes and responsibilities that go with sustained living. Without a fervent commitment to this new mindset and way of being, we could easily vanish as a species. This realization should be enough to light our fire and keep it stoked to create sustainable lives.

Mother Nature's rules and ways of life work across the board, showing us how to manage our relationships, business partnerships, and social/political alliances by its ecological, symbiotic way of making and conserving communities of ever-unfolding diversity.

For our personal and collective economies, nature teaches us the fundamentals for successful work and finances. In the business of living, Nature economically produces, re-greens, reinvents and exchanges a staggering abundance of goods and services, again and again. Ecologic is economic and profuse.

If ever there is a living embodiment of balance and wholeness, it is nature. The precision of how all the different gazillion moving parts on earth coordinate, cooperate, collaborate, communicate, co-create and co-evolve is dazzling and truly miraculous.

Perhaps most importantly, all organisms know who they are instinctively. All organisms know their talents and skills, and what to do with them for their role in the great ecological community we call Earth. Nature knows itself and produces itself. By following natural principles, you find your niche and your own creative and unique gifts. Nature is authentic and on-purpose. By living in your own knowing, you are productive, happy, and efficient, rewarding both yourself and future generations.

4. Nature Is Us

The most vital quality for sustained living which we would not generally identify is being "natural." The absolute sine qua non for sustainability is naturalness—to know and express yourself as nature. This realization reconnects you with the natural world. An unnatural life is unbalanced and, ultimately, unsustainable. Disconnection from the natural world and from our own nature as nature is a primary source of our physical, psychological, and spiritual dis-eases. We now call this sickness "outdoor deprivation disorder."

The easiest and quickest way to remedy this is to go for a walk in nature, often called "the first meditation," because it restores your natural equilibrium. The sustainable life is a call to the nature that you are and to a renewed reconnection of respect and reverence for the environment that will rejuvenate and heal you.

We are born to follow earth's ways because we ourselves are earth creatures. We are born of this earth, by the earth, and for the earth. Originating from the stardust of the cosmos and subsequently evolving into the first cells and into the plants and animals, we are an inextricable part of a vast interconnected unfurling. On this web of life, we have evolved with the essential qualities of all that has preceded us.

The greatest graphic evidence that we share most of nature with ourselves is that when you look at a human DNA molecule alongside the DNA of a palm tree or penguin, it looks virtually the same to the human eye. Look and you will see that we are one with the earth and all of its inhabitants, each mirroring the other in its core components, and yet manifesting in infinite and varied ways.

The most shocking fact that we are inextricably part of nature is that of the trillions of cells that compose us, only 10 percent are inherently human. Our body is literally our earth.

And did you know that the mighty mouse has 90 percent of the same 20,000 genes as a human? And that this same mouse has a brain structure almost exactly the same as ours?

Some might say that because we are emotional beings with a vast range of feelings, nature is not relevant to how we should live. Yet, as we learn more about the fauna and flora of this planet, we know that they have feelings as well. Apes have a well-developed sense of empathy. Plants and flowers are sensitive to the intentions of their human gardeners. Nature may not show happiness, though when the sun comes out, poppies seem ecstatic to me. We've all seen the wagging of a dog's tail when we come home, the frolicking of cats at play, and the wailing of an elephant upon the death of one of its herd. I am sure that all life forms have some level of desire, contentment and fear, though they might be primarily felt through physical sensation and not emotive expression.

No doubt the human species is unique in nature, but then again, every living organism is distinctive. We humans have special skills—but so does a 4,000-year-old Bristlecone Pine, a flying squirrel, an eight armed octopus, and spiders who live 15,000 feet high in the air. Our brainy intelligence for imagining, tool-making and abstract thinking, coupled with the range of emotions, does make us special and yet, at risk. Sustainability for humans is far more complex, full of choices, powers and distractions that divert us from the natural task and focus at hand. The rest of nature instinctively knows how to sustain and unquestioningly follows sustainable ways.

Because we feel that we are entitled, separate, and superior to nature, we have taken sustainability for granted. Sustainability does not have the equivalent gravitas, the same imperative authority and motivation for us as it has for all other natural creatures.

Yet, as natural beings, we possess nature's sustain abilities and green wisdom inherent within us. We do know how to be healthy, live long, re-energize and renew, find peace and fulfillment, produce, collaborate, serve, grow, create, protect, and leave a legacy for future generations. We use the Sustainability Cards to remind us who we are, recognize our inner resources, and remember how to utilize these gifts of nature.

Of all the sustain abilities that we must focus on, once we remember our naturalness, it is knowing yourself and your apotheosis—your divine life purpose. If you know these two core life aspects about yourself, the rest falls into place and sustained living becomes easier.

Who are you and why are you? Ask yourself, what are your gifts, talents and skills? What is your way to embody these abilities as your purpose in life? Apply these three critical questions to every area of life and you will find your ever-greening path.

But we don't seem to know who we are. We get lost in a sea of cultural conditioning for who we should be according to others as we try to follow the conventional story of how to live. The astonishing sustainability of nature is that it knows itself and what to do. Even though we self-reflect and are self-aware, all of the natural world, except for us, is self-knowing. We think we know, but because we know by thinking, we don't really know what pulses through us in every living fiber of our being.

We humans have lost the feel of our natural inclinations and the sustainability instinct. We don't feel the pull of the life force within us which determines the intention, direction and meaning of our lives. We've become divorced from our own selves, our feelings, and body by unnatural, mechanistic and herd-like socialized behavior. The Sustain Yourself Cards assist us in rediscovering our own inner natural way of knowing.

Of course, to some extent, we do know ourselves and what we are meant to do with our lives, but we don't always act on that knowledge. One of the most fundamental natural sustain abilities that goes unobserved because of its obviousness is its activeness. Nature does. Plants and animals don't sit around debating, doubting, and procrastinating. They know what they have to do and they do it. The cards are catalysts and tools for our proaction. Nature is all about what works and it is through actions that we get results.

When you intentionally and actually live in the sustainable way of nature, you experience the manifestation magic of apotheosis—to grow yourself, realize your potentials and reach your destiny and life purpose, the way a redwood tree knows it's a redwood, employs all of its resources, and attains its height, longevity and grandeur.

On your way of apotheosis, you are naturally happy and fulfilled because you are yourself, authentic, uncompromised and unpolluted by false beliefs. When you have a happy heart, you live a healthier and longer life, plain and simple. To achieve this highest state of development and fruition, you create, grow, and produce according to your capabilities, and learn how to keep renewing and regenerating the way a tree recycles itself. On this path, you live a rich existence and contribute to the richness of the world, social and natural. Though there are no guarantees in life, the sustainable way gives you the very best opportunity to live long, prosperously, peacefully and passionately.

Part Three

SUSTAIN YOURSELF CARDS

The Sustainability Game of Life

5. Playing With the Cards

Our inherent sustain abilities are developed and exercised by knowing and absorbing these natural gifts mentally, emotionally sensorily, and by externalizing them through physical expression and action in the world. By playing the Sustainability Game, the Cards educate, give you insight, and evoke sustainable behavior and deeds.

You play with the Sustain Yourself Cards by choosing one or more of them intuitively from the Deck facedown. The cards are to be contemplated and acted upon.

The surprise, synchronicity and symbols of the Cards break you free of old, habitual thinking and move you out of inertia. It's a compelling transformative tool, and it's fun, so you continue to use it and develop your sustain abilities.

THE GAME OF LIFE

Treat sustainability as a game, though a serious game, with yourself. In this "game of life"—as it's about life's basic principles of sustainment—you become more resilient, more focused and resourceful, more reflective and active. You win.

Games always invite mystery and surprise, like the Cards you get, such as the kind of ball the baseball pitcher throws to you. Games are about how you respond to what comes your way and how you play your hand. In our changing world today, we are constantly startled and sometimes taken aback by what life brings us, so this game prepares you for sustaining in revolutionary times. The Cards test your intuitive discernment and creativity to understand their universal meaning for your lot in life.

Games are won or lost depending upon how well you play the game, and in the life game of sustainability, it is how sincerely you embody and act upon the ecological principles that are the Cards. There is no adversary except yourself. The winner is your own sustainability, which carries over into the sustainability of our social and natural environments.

WAYS OF PLAYING THE GAME

In Sustainability, there are many ways to consult the Cards. You can play it alone or with others, frequently as a daily activation practice or occasionally for various specific questions and issues.

Each Card represents one of our key sustain abilities—a fundamental eco-principle for personal, social and environmental conservation and regeneration. By consulting the Cards, nature becomes your coach and mentor. Like nature, which acts and does in contrast to our pondering, Sustainability is purposed for "doing," not just thinking and knowing mentally. Nature gets results.

Consulting the Cards as a guide for insight can be about sustaining yourself and any aspect of your life—personal growth, relationships, love, work, money, health, environment, world conditions, community and more.

The down-to-earth payoff of these inquiries is to act and apply your understanding. This process is known as "intuaction," a hybrid word that means "intuition into action." This is nature's way of being—doing the instinctual.

So, at the conclusion of your "consultation game," determine what you are going to do about it. Doing it establishes whether you sustain or not. The ultimate way of playing the various games is by acting on the Card(s) for self-sustainability and for sustaining your relationships, community, and natural environment.

6. Natural Knowing: Understanding the Cards

To understand the meaning of the green wisdoms, be natural. Utilize the diverse and various ways that follow below by which nature knows itself, in addition to the uniquely human gift of symbolic, imaginative, and analytical thinking.

INTUITION

Nature follows its instincts without doubt. Get in touch with your own instinctual knowing by intuiting the meaning of the Cards. Trust and follow your spontaneous impulses! Even if you read the written definitions and ponder the Cards, it is ultimately your own inner knowing that knows and decides.

KEY PHRASE & CATCHWORDS

All Card descriptions contain a Key Phrase which encapsulates the Card's essential message. Use your intuitive association ability by letting them suggest meaning and action. The written interpretations of the Cards also include Keywords that are meant to spark aha's.

CREATIVITY

Like the inherent and essential creative quality of nature, be creative with the Cards. Play with them in any way that works for you. Look at what they might mean from its colors, its shapes and forms, location in the world, and connection to other parts of the ecosystem and its evolving role. Go beyond the book. Get wild!

SENSORY

Use your own sensory nature to comprehend a Card. Apply your five senses. What is the smell, taste, sound, sight and feel of the Card? Sniff out what the Card means to you using your "wisdom nose." Sound out the Card and what that sound means to you. Get out of your thinking brain and comprehend the Card with all of your intelligences and perceptivity.

EXPRESSIVE

Embody the Card with breath, sound, movement, and emotion. Act it out. By this expressive, kinesthetic intuition, discover new meanings of the Cards and new dimensions of yourself. This process is a "natural yoga" that can bring out the star, the wolf, the Bird of Paradise in you. When we identify and move to nature within ourselves, we create even stronger connections to our world.

IN NATURE

Take your Cards into nature and let the energetic synchronicity of you and the earth reveal your Cards, your awareness and embodiment of them.

INTERDEPENDENCE

Everything in life is interdependent, so as a general principle for reading the Cards, pay attention to the most immediate part(s) of nature's ecology that your Card is connected to and dependent upon.

VIGILANCE (DANGER SIGNS)

All of nature is protective of itself. Watch out and be on guard for the dangers implicit in the nature of the cards. Every card, like every aspect and phenomenon of life, has a red flag, a warning. Everything has some kind of vulnerability. And how you apply the Card has its own problematics—too much or too little, too fast or too slow undermines sustainability. Always pay attention to the potential challenges. Be vigilant.

7. Consultation Games

The many ways of consulting the Cards range from a "Daily One Card Action" process to structured "Four-Card Layouts" to "Question and Answer" free-form consults to more elaborate multi-card exercises. Each is designed for you to become more sustain-able. Experiment and explore by yourself or with others and remember the mantra of "Have Fun, Do Good, Sustain."

"GREEN YOURSELF TODAY" • THE SUSTAIN ABILITY ACTIVATION

Apply the Deck as a sacred ritual to preserve your creative life force. Treat this as spiritual growth, evolutionary, and down-to-earth sustainability "practice."

The natural world is animated and active. Nature Does. Use the Cards as activators by being the cards in action. Via empathy and expression, become one with earth by embodying your natural self through the cards.

Pick a Daily card to Activate yourself or any particular area of your life. This practice will keep you focused, and inform you, energize you, grow you and sustain you. "A Card A Day Keeps Death Away."

You can do this Activation in the following ways, but first pick a card with the INTENTION of embodying it in your life.

Then, you can:

REFLECT on how you are actually living the nature in the Card. This connects you with nature and affirms your natural being.

IMAGINE in your mind's eye taking a journey into the nature in the Card. In fact, your trillions of body cells respond as though you were physically there in nature.

EXPRESS and EMBODY the nature in the Card as you act them out by Moving and Sounding to it. Physically entrain yourself with nature.

TAKE ACTION in your life by serving the function that the nature in the Card suggests.

SITUATE yourself physically, when possible, in nature, where the Card suggests.

"ASK MOTHER NATURE" · EXPLORE, DISCOVER, SUSTAIN

What would Mother Nature say? Ask the Cards any question. "Ask Mother Nature" for insight and inspiration. Nature Knows.

This free-form reading has no rules, no set number of cards, no layout positions. In this Question and Answer process, explore the truth by perhaps more than one question and more than one Card. Your curiosity and creative intuition are required.

A good question to begin using the Cards is to ask the Deck how the Cards can help you become more sustainable. Pick a Card.

The question of questions is "Who Am I?" Ask Mother Nature what's your nature and what's your purpose and path.

"GREEN LEAVES READING" · THE NATURE OF NOW

Cast the the Cards out like leaves and read them like tea leaves to see what comes up. Using your intuition, read the arrangement, or just the Cards that appear face up. Or simply select one or more from the pile of "leaves" to synchronistically symbolize the present moment, the nature of now and your own nature now.

"THE SUSTAIN ABILITY JOURNEY" · SELF-NAVIGATION

Walking the green path of sustainability requires various mandatory navigation qualities, which are indicated below. The nature of sustainability is a progressive, evolutionary journey that takes you from your present situation in life to your "leaves of legacy."

Pick a Card for each:

- Your Present Sustain Ability...
- Your Energy for the Journey...
- Your Creativity...
- Your Balance...
- Your Motivation and Interest...
- Your Joy and Fulfillment...
- Your Personal Authenticity...

- Your Right Livelihood...
- Your Relationships and Partnerships...
- Your Growth...
- Your Challenge...
- Your Social and Environmental Contribution...
- Your Legacy...

"SYNERGY" · THE WHOLE ENERGIZED YOU

The path of sustainability is Holistic, requiring the use of mind, emotion, body, spirit and action in the world. In this comprehensive way of being, all parts of you are integrated and catalyzed — synergized!

Pick a Card for each:

- Your Mental Clarity...
- Your Emotional Expressiveness...
- Your Physical Energy...

- Your Spiritual Growth...
- Your Worldly Success...

Read the synergy of how each of these aspects of yourself work together. Taken together, these Cards indicate your personal ecology and whether they are symbiotic and mutual (working and sharing together for mutual benefit) or out of balance.

"STATE OF THE WORLD" · SUSTAINABLE ENVIRONMENTS

Pick a Card for the sustainable condition of your own world and/or the world at large:
- Your Relationship(s) / International Relations...
- Your Work / World Economy...
- Your Money / Global Finances...
- Your Home / Country...
- Your Environment (Social, Work, Family and/or Community) / Nature...

In these Readings of more than just one Card, take a look at how they work together or not. Do the Cards taken as a whole indicate a sustainable ecology?

TERRA FIRMA FOUR-CARD BEDROCK CONSULTATIONS

"THE FOUR ESSENTIALS OF PRODUCTIVITY" · Sustain by Producing

Pick a Card for each:
- Your Skills... Each aspect of nature knows itself and what it's good at.
- Your Work... Nature knows what it's supposed to do.
- Your Action... Nature acts and does it.
- Your Re-doing... Nature repeats it.

"THE FOUR ELEMENTS" · The Elemental You Game

Select a Card for each of the four elements:
- Your Fire nature...
- Your Water nature...
- Your Earth nature...
- Your Air nature...

(You can categorize the Cards by the Elements, e.g., Air cards include flying creatures, clouds, weather, skies, etc. and pick a Card from each of those Elemental groupings).

"THE FOUR SEASONS" · Recycling Yourself

Choose a Card for each of the four seasons:
- Your Spring nature (what to start)...
- Your Summer nature (what to maintain)...
- Your Fall nature (what to harvest)...
- Your Winter nature (what to rest and plan for)...

"THE FOUR DIRECTIONS" · Your Inner Family

Select a Card for each of the four directions:
- Your East Rising-Sun Child (Inner Child)...
- Your West Setting-Sun Sage (Inner Grandmother/father)...
- Your South Ocean Mother (Inner Feminine)...
- Your North Sky Father (Inner Masculine)...

BIOSPHERE CONSULTATIONS

Biosphere consults are Five-Card Layouts that are organized around the five basic "Domains" of nature. These readings give you the sum of your own personal ecosystem.

For these, divide the Deck into the five "Domains" of the biosphere: ELEMENTAL, MINERAL, PLANT, ANIMAL, HUMAN.

(Note that some classifications of the Cards cross over into more than one Domain and some aspects of nature are now their own domain like bacteria, but these kinds of new classifications are kept traditional and generalized here.)

Elemental

Atom	Earth Changes	Polarity	Waves
Breath	Fire	Rainbow	Weather
Cells	Gases	River	Web
Channel	Horizon	Spiral	Wild Card
Clouds	Lake	Stars	Winter
Darkness	Lightning	Sun	
Desert Wind	Nothing	Sunset	
Earth	Ocean	Water	

Mineral

Cave	Gold	Silicon	Stone
Diamond	Mountain	Silver	
Flower and Rock	Plateau	Soil	

Plant

Algae	Food	Palm Tree	Roots
Bacteria	Fungus	Peapod	Seeds
Compost	Grasslands	Pollination	Tulips
Fall Leaves	Jungle	Redwood Tree	Wheat

Animal

Ant	Dogs	Hive	Sheep
Bear	Dolphin	Horses	Snake
Caterpillar	Eagle	Leapin' Lemur	Turtle
Chameleon	Egg	Moon Wolf	Whale
Cheetah and Sunflower	Elephant and Saturn	Primates	
Dead Fish	Geese	Reef Fish	
	Head to Head	Rodents	

Human

Ancestor	Eucalyptus Man	Hand	Senses
Arrowhead	Face to Face	Heart	Sex
Babies	Fetus	Man	Wild Woman
Brain	Footprints	Mother	Youth
Danger	Greening Man	Parent	
DNA	Green Road	Purification	

"WHAT'S MY NATURE?" • YOUR BIOSPHERIC SELF

This assessment is for understanding who you are from a complete biospheric perspective.

Divide the Cards into the Five Domains of the Biosphere.

Pick a Card for each Domain:

- Your Elemental Self (Elemental cards)...
- Your Mineral Self (Mineral cards)...
- Your Plant Self (Plant cards)...
- Your Creature Self (Animal cards)...
- Your Human Self (Human cards)...

After looking at each Card and their meaning for you regarding the position they are in, evaluate how they all comprise a viable ecology of you.

"ECO-SUSTAINABILITY"

Use the Five-card Biosphere Domains to get a complete map of how to sustain yourself and/or any one aspect of your life, including the environment, itself.

Pick a Card for your Sustainability from each Domain:

- Elemental...
- Mineral...
- Plant...
- Animal...
- Human...

After analyzing the individual Cards, what does your whole Biosphere look like? How sustainable is it as an ecosystem?

GROUP SYNERGY "WHAT DO YOU BRING TO THE JUNGLE?"

Each participant in your group picks one Card from the entire Deck for what they bring to the "Jungle" (the nature and ecology of your group).

Preferably, each participant talks about their Card and themselves and how that contributes to your group ecosystem.

Place all the Cards chosen in the Five Biosphere Domains. Evaluate the synergy of your ecosystem.

Part Four

SUSTAIN YOURSELF CARD INTERPRETATIONS

The 101 Eco-Principles

The eco-principles, or sustain-abilities, are alphabetically arranged and are represented by the pictorial cards.

As you read about these abilities, ask yourself how you can enact them in your life. Deeds do speak louder than words. Sustaining yourself and world demands action. Sow these seeds of consciousness and watch your life grow and flourish.

The compressed write-ups of the sustain-abilities contain a Key Phrase to trigger "Intuaction" on your behalf.

The GREEN LEAF on the backside of each card is the first and most imperative eco-principle of self-sustainability. It represents your Connection with Nature to Be Natural, Protect the Earth, and Follow Mother Nature's ways. You are the Earth, Keep it Green and Green yourself.

KEY: LIVE NATURALLY.

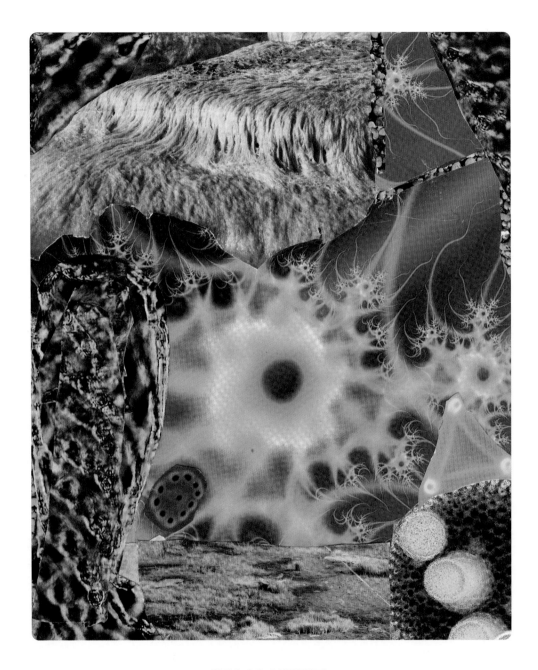

KEY: GO OUTSIDE.

ALGAE — Light

Like algae, earth's first photosynthesizers, get out into the Natural Light (You need two hours of daylight every day to be healthy). Eat plants full of light and energy. Breathe in the oxygen of algae, green plants and trees. Go to the park. Hike in the Forest. Walk on the beach. Inhale the sun. For the more adventurous, Gaze at the Sun.

KEY: DO IT BETTER WITH AGE.

ANCESTOR — Aging

Your Biology is changing and by consciously growing yourself with aging and seasoning, you reach full maturity. Call upon your experienced wisdom to produce and perform more effectively. With age, you are more authentic, happy and free. Mitigate entropy and breakdowns by copious amounts of water like the sponge, a human forerunner, and by a healthy mind that doesn't sweat the small stuff. Conserve energy like the ancient Bristlecone Pine. Think longevity. Be a Sage and Mentor, healed and whole. Respect and Invoke your ancestors, forerunners, and elders.

KEY: WORK WITH OTHERS.

ANT — Collaboration

Cooperate and Collaborate in Communion to build Community. It's about Teaming. You cannot do it alone! Organize a Social System and Division of Labor that works. Like the Industrious ant, Do Your Work. March to the Rules of the Road. Keep lines of Communication Open and Active. Use your Awareness antennae and wisdom nose to Smell your way along, and Pheromones to Attract your mates.

Devise devices and make tools to assist you implement your productions. Invent avatars that extend your power for an easier and more secure life. Project and Propel yourself into the future. Determine your direction. With red-hot ambition, drive, and foresight, intentionalize where you want to go. Gather the means to hit your target. Use your influence and instruments responsibly because they can destroy.

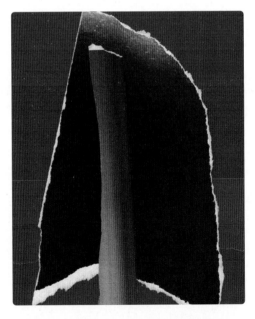

KEY: FOCUS WITH INTENTION.

ATOM — In Motion

The chemical base of you and of all matter is atomic, which in perpetual motion gives you the ability to go beyond limitations, beyond belief, senses, prediction, physicality. Your atomic nature is infinitesimally small, ultimately immeasurable, ridiculously quirky, shockingly unreal, unimaginably complex, fiercely independent, and not. Anything is possible and nothing is certain, so keep hopping and bopping. Be the Quantum Surprise on the move. Anything goes!

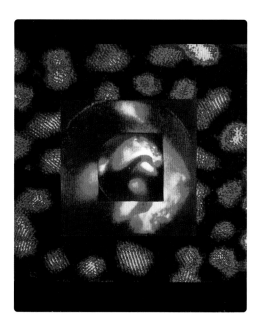

KEY: DO THE IMPOSSIBLE.

BABIES — Learning

You are born to learn and keep learning. With your primal drive to know, assimilate how to be a human and Earth being. Every day, learn something new and grow. With an open, beginner's mindset, new information is processed for new behaviors, knowledge, skills, and values from anywhere, anyone at anytime. Let curiosity lead your life. And laugh (babies do 500 times a day) to last.

KEY: LEARN TO LIVE AND KNOW TO GROW.

BACTERIA — Sustainability

Your body is mostly bacteria—the oldest sustainable life success on earth. As bacteria and like bacteria, make everything and every situation food, energy source and opportunity. Convert stumbling blocks into building blocks. Amazingly prolific (40 million bacteria in a gram of soil), bacteria are indispensable, absolutely cooperative, and communicative; they collaborate and multiply, innovate, adapt, and circumvent limitations, even those imposed by nature!

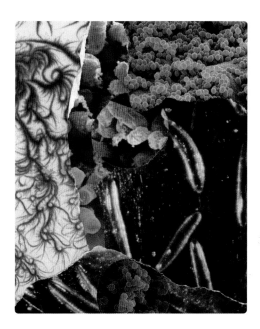

KEY: RE-SOURCE EVERYTHING.

KEY: SLEEP WELL.

BEAR — Sleep

Sleep for restoration, rejuvenation, health, mood, performance.
Ensure good sleep by being a bear of activity—move, work, eat, play.
Do all your duties so you are prepared for time out and for the future.
Like the solitary, hibernating bear, make your sleeping place a comfy
cave that is dark, coolish, unwired, safe, uninterruptible. Dream.

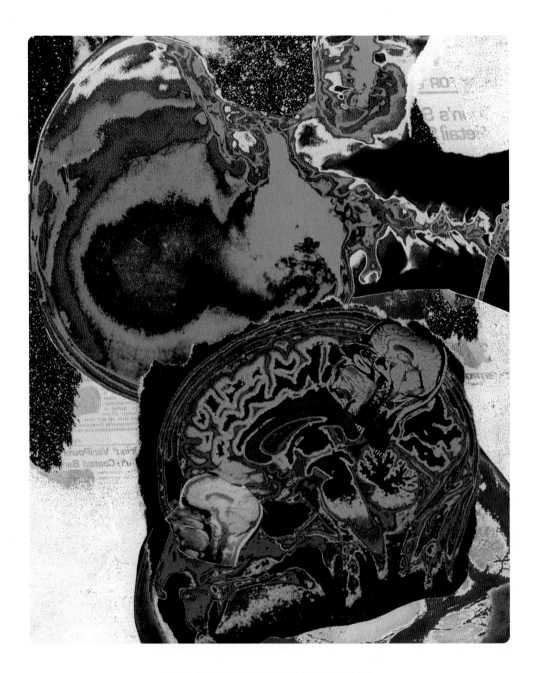

KEY: MIND YOUR WHOLE BRAIN.

BRAIN — Self-Governance

Use the powers of your total brain in balance with open mind and positive thinking. Integrate forebrain intention, vision, foresight and focus with left brain analysis; with right brain creativity; with emotional forebrain intuition; and with alpha wave meditative equanimity to decide, guide, clarify, invent, influence navigate, self-determine. Do not overthink.

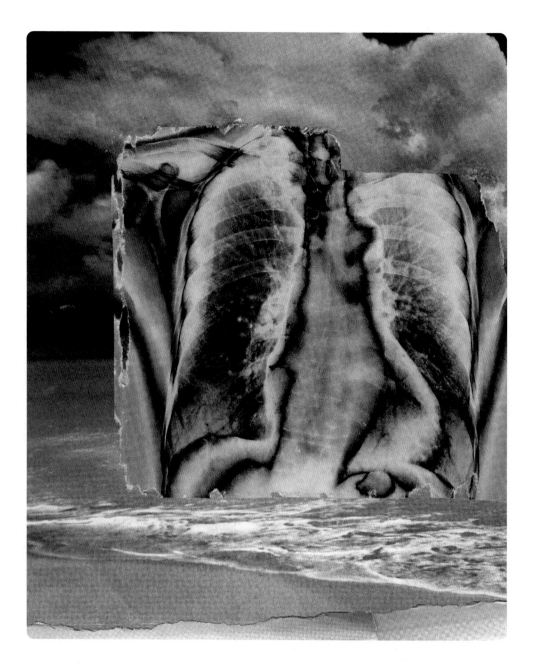

KEY: BREATHE TO LIVE.

BREATH — Oxygenation

Aerobicize to purify and re-grow new brain and body cells. Oxygen deprivation is the source of our ills, so swift, deep breathing while moving is your quickest and cleanest renewable way to heal and re-energize. Powerful respiration brings inspiration. Breathe outdoor air, inhale negative ions, exhale to rest and restore.

CATERPILLAR — Transformation

Like a caterpillar on its way, life is at all times a process of transformation to the apotheosis of realized potential. In constant preparation and maturation, which takes learning, growing, persevering, and risking, go onwards, one do-able step after another, row by row, changing and unfolding day by day—"kaizen." Make progress. Evolve.

KEY: BECOME THE BUTTERFLY.

CAVE — Investigation

Caves are openings, allowing for access and egress. Don't close or block channels of discovery and opportunity. Enter the portal within to explore inner resources and streams of possibility. Inside of you is a sanctuary, a place of refuge, an interior home that is you, inviolate and sacred. Penetrate to the truth, dig into what is hidden, even to what you disown and deny about yourself.

KEY: TUNNEL TO TRUTH.

CELLS — Renewal and Self-Creation

Cells (all 100 trillion in the average human body) are the smallest organic basis of you. These short-lived, self-contained cells give you life, then die, and then live again. The repetition of this death and rebirth process means you are in constant replication and reproduction. Cells will even commit suicide for you when damaged or starved. Feed your cells with nourishing food, no-stress positivity, and exercise to restore, remember and renew yourself.

KEY: FOLLOW THE GOLDEN RULE OF BIOLOGY: CELLS TREAT YOU HOW YOU TREAT THEM.

CHAMELEON — Adapt-ability

Fit into your world. Like a chameleon, adapt and adjust to your environment. You are multidimensional, change-able and adapt-able to habituate to any circumstance. Conform, commingle, connect, communicate, co-evolve—continuously sensitive to ever-changing environs, people, situations, possibilities. Revamp, rework, restyle, redefine. The Flex-able never get bent out of shape.

KEY: SHAPESHIFT ON DEMAND.

KEY: IMPULSE IS YOUR WAY TO SOURCE.

CHANNEL — Life Force

You are a living expression of the Great Spirit as you open the portal and passage to transmit and receive from the source of higher power to guide your life. Be a medium and move as one with the Prime Mover. Find the spirit frequency and feel the current for fulfilling your soul contract. create with the creative life force. Do what gives you energy. Feel the intuitive impulse and follow it!

KEY: BE THE BEST YOU CAN.

CHEETAH & SUNFLOWER — Aspiration

Strive to your finest and be on top of your game. Move swiftly, make your mark, and achieve your peak expression. Grow to the highest. Hunt the outstanding. Pursue personal excellence and beauty to be the foremost and preeminent. Set the standard. Know what you're good at and perfect it.

KEY: MAKE IT UP.

CLOUDS — Manifestation

Out of nothing comes something. Yours is the power to magically materialize. Alchemist of airy thoughts with fiery spirit and watery moods and space to be free, create and change new and different. Nothing set and fixed, you are a transitioning verb in motion—gently and easily moving with an imagination leading to another until it rains returns.

COMPOST — Recycling

There is no waste in Nature. Everything has value. Whatever you've done is fertilizer and opportunity for new growth. Transform setbacks into success, mistakes into learning, sorrow into purification, oppression into liberation, sickness into health, confusion into clarity, disappointment into understanding. Do not trash and deny. It's all energy: reuse, return, reform. Digest, decompose, and process your garbage into gold.

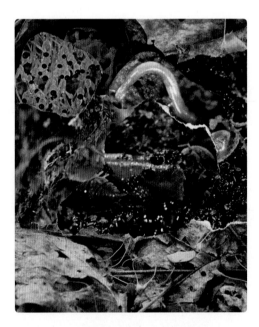

KEY: TURN AND CONVERT.

DANGER — Vigilance

From pests to pestilence, mites to malaria, criminals to cancer, poisons to toxins, contamination to pollution, invasion to decay, you are threatened. Watch out, be careful. Live clean, healthy, sanitary. Take precaution and preventive care, but with no paranoia and don't obsess. There are more germs on your body than people in the U.S.

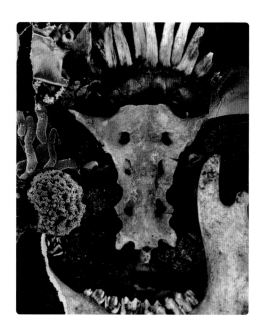

**KEY: IF IT DOESN'T KILL,
IT STRENGTHENS.**

DARKNESS — Intuition

In the dark, it's all a Mystery. Trust your intuitions and feel your way. Use blindness to develop other senses and the extra-sensory. Do not fear or judge the blackness. Probe the unenlightened secret parts of yourself that are hidden. Meditate. At night, relax, sleep, let go. Pay attention to your dreams—the Unknown reveals itself in dreams.

KEY: CLOSE YOUR EYES TO SEE.

DEAD FISH — Death

No life without death. Accept endings. Grieve through your tears and they will rain new life. All eventually decays and breaks down. Release and Compost what is dead to live again. Renew and revitalize yourself by dying into sleep, time out, change, completion, stopping. Stagnate to regenerate, but if you're feeling stuck, die to the situation, push forth, and break free. Don't pollute and kill.

KEY: DIE TO LIVE.

KEY: SING YOUR SONG.

DESERT WIND — Sound

In open expanses, there is wind—a vibration and wave which is sound and a frequency that is replicated throughout Nature as the roar of ocean, waterfalls, rain, pulsations of the heart. This pink noise fluctuation is a sign of health. Hum and make noise with a voice that throbs with natural rhythm and breath. Air out your windpipe.

KEY: SHINE YOUR LIGHT.

DIAMOND — Adamant

Get crystal clear about your value and how you shine. Believe in your radiance! Diamond hard resolved and committed to your light, it takes time, work, pressure, and patience to be a gem. Endure and persevere with vision, intention and crystalline integrity and boundaries that cannot be penetrated and compromised get you results and payoffs.

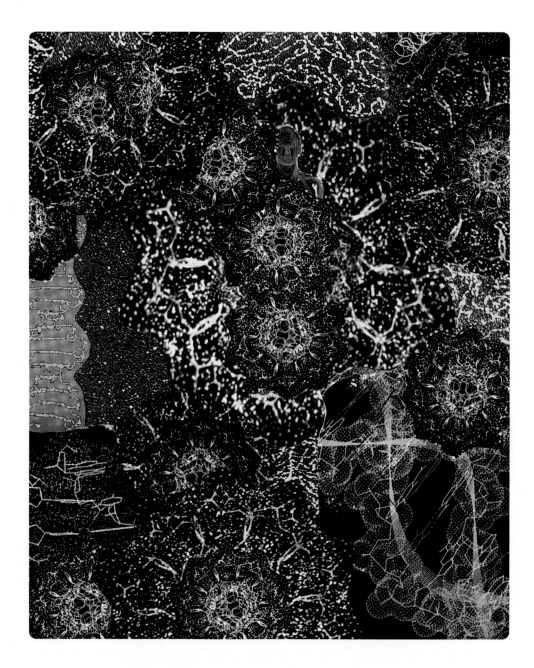

KEY: MANAGE YOUR INHERENT TENDENCIES.

DNA — Memory

Inheritor of the vast treasury of evolutionary history, Remember all of your resources and gifts. You are born with genes and genius with eons-old earth wisdom that crosses all the domains and species of nature and human cultures, races and geography. Know the traits of your own immediate family DNA, but realize that it's dynamic, for you are changing and evolving in this very epigenetic moment. You are not a victim—or victorious —simply by predetermined ancestry.

DOGS — Trust

Be trusting and trustworthy, faithful and dedicated to your relationships. Speak your Truth and express your feelings. Bark out, when you must, but let go of disagreements. Have a short memory. Follow the lead. Guard your home and family with ferocity and show great affection for loved ones. Socialize and run with your pack.

KEY: BE LOYAL.

DOLPHIN — Play

Choose playfulness the way dolphins did in their migration to the sea. Ride the emotional waves with Joy. Jump and spin, dive, and streak. Enjoy the sensual, sexual, and gregarious companionship that dolphins express in their communal social life. Revel in the rich acoustic world of sounds and cosmic song. Feel the vibe, heal the wounded, surf your wave, swim to love.

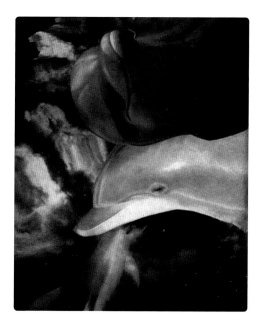

KEY: HAVE FUN, GO DOLPHIN.

EAGLE — Vision

Eye of the Eagle, see afar as a visionary, yet maintain focus and strike with unerring accuracy. Survey from the heights. Look into the doable future with a discerning eye. Always in the hunt of your quest, don't lose touch with your high-minded intention. Take flight. Go the distance.

KEY: SEE THE GOAL, MAKE THE GOAL.

EARTH — Diversity

Earth is abundantly diverse, which enables its astonishing creativity. The mixing of variation naturally originates new organisms. Multiplicity multiplies and change changes. Choose variety, difference, heterogeneity and combine them for best results. You are inextricably interdependent, always part of the wholeness, and one with all other life. Trust the foreign; it's just a hidden part of you in another guise and form.

KEY: SYNERGIZE FOR SUCCESS.

KEY: YOU ARE FOREWARNED.

EARTH CHANGES — Upheaval

Stress, Pressure and tension lead to sudden shakeup and rupture of the old status quo and balance by a release of energy that shocks, displaces, disrupts, and destroys. Radical reorganization ensues, even death. Often Gradual until extinction, prepare or prevent seismic events on their way. Watch your eco-footprint on Nature. Realize that you are a behemoth, perhaps an alien on this planet and that the biggest agent of earth-change is you, the Human.

KEY: MAKE THE BREAK.

EGG — Spring Birth

Rebirth and restart yourself. Begin a new life cycle. Spring forth and emerge. Show up, be seen, present yourself. Coming out and bringing out demands bravery and trust as you separate from the known and secure. It takes Labor and energy to break out, be free, and assume responsibility.

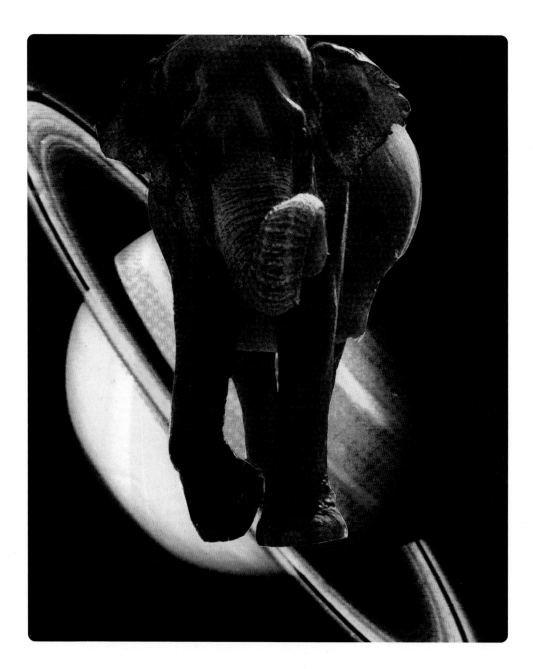

KEY: KEEP IT TOGETHER.

ELEPHANT & SATURN — Gravity

You have pull, gravitas, the power to coalesce and hold. Live elephant-large and wise to be a magnate, and the world of opportunity will gravitate to you, to your ring of power and sphere of influence. With this force of attraction, you are connected and grounded with the staying strength to lead, organize, and build that which endures and serves.

EUCALYPTUS MAN — Guardian

With shield and club, you are endowed with responsibility for guarding against any war on life. You are a steward for ensuring the safety and well-being of yourself, others, and environment. Defend and deter against those who aggress upon the right to freedom of expression. To be a life-keeper is your sacred obligation. Keep trees standing. Keep people growing.

KEY: PROTECT AND POLICE.

FACE TO FACE — Love

Life is relationship. Relate, engage, empathize and most of all, love. With intimacy, openness, and vulnerability, connect with your fellow feelers. You are a social creature that needs friends, partners, allies, community, and family. Love is the bond that keeps us together, safe, and sustainable. Touch and be touched. Eye to eye and heart to heart, your word is good. Follow the Golden Rule.

KEY: COMMUNICATE TO COMMUNICATE.

FALL LEAVES — Completion

Autumn is your season for completing and finishing a growth cycle. Get your work done, then release, drop it and let go. Acknowledge and appreciate the golden richness that you manifested. Like a falling leaf, surrender yourself to conserve life so that you survive the winter and thrive in coming times. Prune back. Reduce your load. Get lean.

KEY: SACRIFICE FOR THE FUTURE.

FETUS — New

An ever-changing process of preparation and development, life from moment to moment is always new and novel. Look anew and do new things. Be open, opportunistic, intuitive, and positive to realize the unborn, latent potentials and possibilities of unpredictable growth. Look forward and make up the future. It's all an adventure of wonder. Excitement is in the air. Feel the zeitgeist. When the time is right, appear.

KEY: SEE THE WOW, BE THE WOW.

KEY: UNLEASH THE VOLCANO WITHIN.

FIRE — Volcanic

Start a Fire to purify and cleanse, to transform, to catalyze, to heat up, to enlighten, to bring warmth. Ignite, burst, erupt, and explode with what's burning in you. Get hot and get it out. Be spontaneous. sizzle, sear and flash with passion, fervor, anger, desire. Express your revolutionary revelations. Expose the fire in your belly. Turn on, get cooking, you are dynamic and energized. Take the heat for the truth.

KEY: CO-CREATE.

FLOWER & ROCK — Co-Evolution

Most minerals evolved with the growing biomass including flowers like the exotic Strelitzia, so everything you do impacts on everything else. All others' actions affect and Influence your growth. As things change, you are changing and your DNA is transforming. Diversify and evolve with the life that is adjusting around you. Soft and hard can get along. Adapt, harmonize, grow.

KEY: YOU ARE WHAT YOU EAT.

FOOD — Nourishment

Eat Natural — whole, organic, unprocessed foods, and include plenty of vegetables, fruits, and grains to nourish a healthy, happy long life. Make it tasty! Don't lose your appetite and your hunger, it's your life force, but eat less, eat local, eat slow. Taste and chew. Food is medicine. Food is energy. Food rules.

FOOTPRINTS — Information

The sands of time expose the past and reveal the future. Know who you are by where you come from. Dig Deep to find the stones and bones of your ancestors and their ways. Excavate and analyze the artifacts you have inherited to know the path you are on. Gather Intelligence to live intelligently. What bones (Legacy) will you leave? Your footprint on the world has impact on the future.

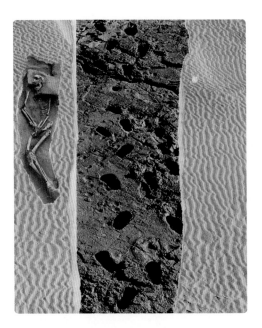

KEY: GO BACK TO GO AHEAD.

FUNGUS — Decomposition

There is no creation without destruction, Decompose and disintegrate things like fungi so that new production, expansion, and mushrooming can begin. Be a quiet, undercover revolutionary to facilitate the process of purification, recovery, and renewal. Undertake the necessary dirty work that is unglamorous, unseemly, and undervalued.

KEY: BREAK IT DOWN TO BUILD IT UP.

GASES — Expansion

Expand and extend freely to fill available space, opportunity, and necessity. spread your power to facilitate and fuel. Envelop to safe-guard, shield, insulate, and screen. With subtlety and gentle influence, do your unseen work that pervades, impacts and effects. Take great care and responsibility that you don't pollute with toxic behavior and hazardous, inflammatory thoughts and speech.

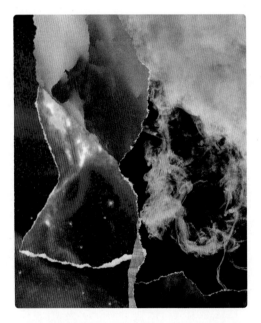

KEY: PRESSURE, PUSH, PREVAIL.

GEESE — Migration

Get up and move! A body in motion stays in motion and is alive. Be mobile. Get up to speed and soar with momentum. Move on and find your home on Earth. Migrate to what sustains you. Trust your inner compass and homing instinct. Travel with your tribe to get inspiration and perspective. Journey to learn and know yourself. Get away and go places.

KEY: MOVEMENT IS LIFE.

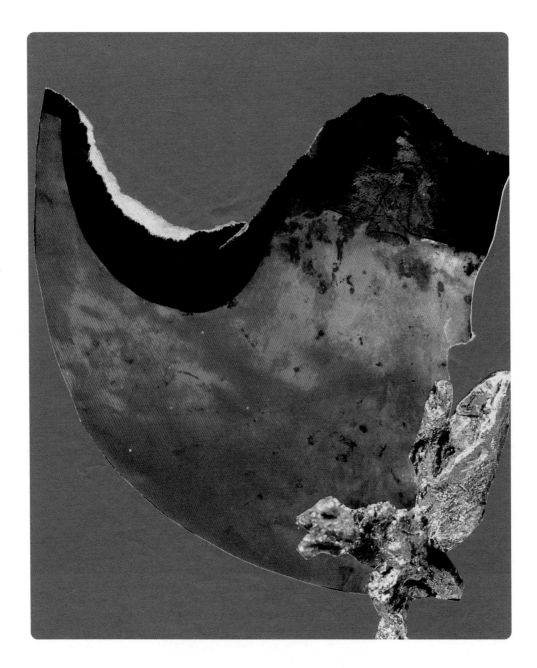

KEY: BEND AND DON'T BREAK.

GOLD — Flex-Ability

Gold is precious because of its "both/and" quality. It is colorful, beautiful, and practical. Gold is both ductilely malleable and imperviously hard. It is attractive, lustrous, and able to withstand stress, pressure, and hammering. You are the rare standard of outstanding distinction and sought-after value.

KEY: SHARE THE WEALTH.

GRASSLANDS — Provide

You are a biome source of plenty to support, feed, and supply. Abundant and bountiful, yield and give your riches to those in need. Be generous, charitable, benevolent, magnanimous, altruistic. Open, public-spirited, unpossessive, and unterritorial, let everyone win and benefit. Contribute to the common good. Find comfort and softness for home and restoration.

KEY: BE THE SEASONS.

GREENING MAN — Renewal

Greening Man is a mythic figure throughout human history that represents the eternal spring of perpetual renewal. Green yourself — resurrect, revitalize, restart, and rejuvenate to remain. Re, Re, Re your life. Follow the green way of Nature by acting on what energizes you! Grow Young by living the cycles of Nature for recycling yourself.

GREEN ROAD — Path

Follow the eco-spiritual path. Stay present and focused on the green walk of sustainability. Revere and be one with the Earth as your Church and temple. Nature is your Sanctuary, wisdom guide and inspiration. Reach your destiny by feeding on pure, clean, renewable energy. Trust and act on the impulse that moves and motivates you. Seek your natural rhythm, uncontaminated by any toxic mental conditioning.

KEY: GO ECO!

HAND — Capability

You've got the capability for life in your hands and to handle things. Lend a helping hand and a guiding hand to go hand in hand with others in a hands-on and sometimes hands off way. Receive with an open hand. Let your hands do the talking and the walking. You've got the touch, the tools and technology for healing, discovering, inventing, and making.

KEY: TALENT IS AT HAND.

HEAD TO HEAD — Opposition

We live in a colliding world of opposition and competition. The battle of life is a natural part of co-existence and co-evolution. Know when to stand and when to charge. Contest makes you stronger and determines your place in the world. See conflict and rivals as a way of growing yourself and realizing your potential. Value the Noble Adversary. Play the game. Losing makes you more resilient and resourceful. Watch out for battling solely because of a headstrong idea and ideology.

KEY: COMPETE.

HEART — Health

Like sap moving through a plant, stay healthy to pump, move and circulate your vital fluids. Insure clear passages and arteries that transport life. Maintain the beat by physical exercise, breathing, nutritious diet, and inner peace. Feel your own pulse and empathize with the heartfelt feelings of others. Think with your heart. Move to what makes your heartbeat. Have the heart to follow your heart.

KEY: LIVE WITH HEART.

KEY: MAKE YOUR HOME A HOME.

HIVE — Home

Care for Earth, your home of homes. Be at home—your right natural environment, social ecology, and physical space. Make your home built for your needs as a shelter, gathering spot, studio, office, restorative refuge, temple, and hive of life. Be efficient, requiring no more than what is secure, sustainable, and practical. Design your residence to be attractive and comfortable. Structure, organize, architect, and feng-shui it.

KEY: PIONEER.

HORIZON — Limitation-less

There are limits. Edges and borders restrict your freedom. You can only go so far and then necessity demands stopping. But the life-imperative to evolve and explore requires you find a new way. By losing sight of the shore, discover the depths of yourself. Dare to innovate. Take the leap of faith. Trust the unknown. Believe in imagination.

KEY: RUN YOUR RACE.

HORSES — Freedom

Exercise your independence and the power of self-determination. Break free to autonomy. Follow your own lead. Gallop with your gang to the creative, original, and unrestricted heartbeat of the life force. Jump the fences of limitation and corrals of conventional living. Be true to your own will. Get wild!

JUNGLE — Creativity

You are composed of trillions of cells and billions of brain neurons in constant production and reproduction. Live up to your bio-heritage and create, create, create again and again and again with the jungle of opportunities and resources that you have. You are rich, lush, and fecund beyond measure. Think and act copious, plentiful, profuse, and bountiful with spontaneity. Jump on the possibilities. There's method in the madness of diversity and quantity.

KEY: LIVE PROLIFICALLY.

LAKE — Self-Knowing

Who are you? The lake is a mirror of all that you are. Contain, keep, hold, catch and maintain your original face—the starry skies of your origins and aspirations, and the moonbeams of your feelings and attractions. Renew yourself in the basin of reflection and refreshment. Accept, receive, and see the truth. No denial. Meditate and muse on your path, purpose, and right livelihood.

KEY: RE-VIEW TO RE-COGNIZE.

LEAPIN' LEMUR — Joy

Lift your spirits and celebrate. Enlighten up with enthusiasm and wonder! Have fun and play. Defy the grave and bounce to the spotlight. Lose weight and sense of heaviness. Aerobicize. Raise your standards. Move up, upgrade, jump with leaps and bounds to rise above the same old stuff. Refuse limitation and those who take you down. Bounce back, rebound, and rally from setbacks. Ennoble and enjoy.

KEY: DANCE TO LIFE!

LIGHTNING — Ignition

Awaken, alert and aware, come alive! Be an electric firebrand—kindle, trigger, excite, stimulate, set afire, spark the passion, jump-start desire. instigate and inflame. Get a move on and take charge with the life force that thunders, enlightens, and enlivens. reveal and revolutionize. Swiftly, now, act with the urgency of impulse, do it and exclaim! No pre-meditation, no doubt, no hesitancy.

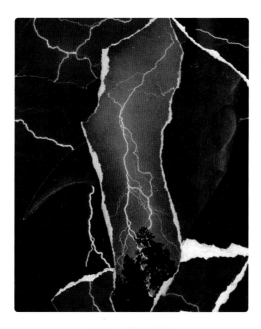

KEY: INITIATE!

KEY: FATHER AND LEAD.

MAN — Imagination

Visualize and conceive in ideal images. Imagine a mental plan and solution for the future. Use pure, universal truths to inspire and inform a way to the realization of perfection. Lead as a living example of wisdom, vision, and impeccability. Father, originate, create, author, sculpt, invent, architect, form and found your progeny, projects, and life purpose. Watch out for cold intellectual, impersonal, judgmental behavior with little tolerance and compassion.

KEY: TRAVEL THE NIGHT.

MOON WOLF — Night

Your peak time is at night to magnetize and attract. Express, howl and shine your desire. With your pack, your tribe, and family make your bonding and gather together at moonrise. Transmit your highest intentions and territorial rights. Exalt, sing, move, meditate, pray, and write to the primal calling of the evening's clear channel. In the winter's cold, hunt down your dreams to bare the bone. call home to your ancestors and spirit guides.

KEY: PRODUCE, PROVIDE, PRESERVE, PARENT.

MOTHER — Creation

Born of this Earth, you are a Mother Earth, yourself. Within you is the power of creation. You are cornucopia, birthing a harvest of plenty and abundance to feed and provide sustenance and growth. Materialize and manifest your babies, businesses, brainstorms and heart stirrings with love, nurturing, and compassion.

MOUNTAIN — Amass

Build up, accumulate, and aggregate. Be a prominent peak, stand out and be visible. Become the highest, most elevated you can achieve. Collect and gather experience upon experience to build yourself into a massive life that attracts and inspires. Defy the valleys and seek the majestic. Set your goals high and be ambitious with planning and work. Onwards and upwards, keep going. Defy gravity and the grave.

KEY: LIVE LARGE.

NOTHING — Openness

Most everything is nothing, almost 75 percent of the universe. Don't try so hard to get something that isn't anything. Don't hold your ground because nothing is solid. Give yourself space, call for a time out. go blank with no agenda, no plan. Most of what we see and think is not. Life is run by the hidden and invisible. Keep an open mind and open heart. Live spacious.

KEY: DO NOT.

OCEAN — Receptive

You are a Mother Ocean, source of life. Your power of receptivity generates and creates. In receiving, you give. Absorbing and taking in, you dissolve and solve, transport, and transform. Drop into being low, soft, and deep. Accept and welcome with openness—no judgment, no repulsion, no blocking. Take it all in. Without effort, allow life to happen. Relax. Let go. Float along.

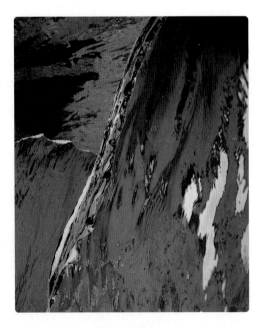

KEY: YIELD.

PALM TREE — Optimization

Everything about a palm tree is useful, as are you. Resource yourself. Nothing is waste and wasted. Be eco-nomic and eco-efficient. Maximize each and every part of you to feed, protect, shelter, transport, contain, and artfully adorn. Exotic and useful in various environments, develop all your potentials and diversify.

KEY: FULFILL.

KEY: EDUCATE, EDUCATE, EDUCATE.

PARENT — Teaching

Nurture, grow and empower the young and others in need of physical support, and emotional, social and mental development. Share your life wisdom, skills, and values. With a loving touch, patience, and compassion, be a role model. Live how you want your child to live. Lead by example. The future is in your hands and heart.

PEAPOD — Ergonomics

Design your work and living space so that they fit and work for your needs, functions, and purposes. Create structures and organize systems that provide the best health and security for growth and performance. Be eco-efficient—shape and construct to use no more space, resources and energy than required. Present yourself and your productions in an attractive, sustainable, recyclable packaging. Standardize your standards so they are reproducible and reliable with quality control.

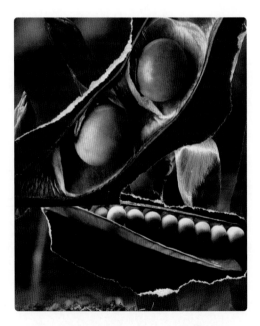

KEY: ECOLOGIC IS ECONOMIC.

PLATEAU — Evenness

Follow the middle way of equanimity and equilibrium. Avoid extremes. Stay even-tempered, stable, constant and consistent. Maintain and continue at the same level and rate. Stay the course and be regular. You've attained and now maintain a rhythm and pace you can sustain. Keep on with persistence and patience. Be at peace, no struggle, no drama, no trauma. Turn boredom into meditation.

KEY: STEADY IT GOES.

POLARITY — Balance

You can't have one without the other. For every north there is a south. For every action there is an opposite and equal reaction. Know the stronger your magnetic influence, the greater the repulsion. To live whole, integrated, and complete, hold to the polar opposites. Maintain dynamic equilibrium by doing the converse of the usual and habitual. Be at variance yet unified, contrasting yet continuous. Do what balances you.

KEY: EMBRACE THE "BOTH-AND."

POLLINATION — Symbiosis

You are a go-between trader of transactions that gives and receives what you and others need to the advantage of all in a win/win exchange. Living in mutual dependence, you are as indispensable to others as others are to you. Buy and sell. Produce and procure. Make deals, barter, swap, negotiate. Communicate to make commerce and community. Market and go to your market.

KEY: I NEED YOU AND YOU NEED ME.

PRIMATES — Sociability

You cannot live without friends, without belonging to a family or community. Find your tribe and your familiars. band and bond together. Befriend companions, playmates, workmates, associates, sisters, brothers, kindred spirits, confidants, parents. Be gregarious, outgoing, and extroverted. Monkey around. Engage, entertain, and empathize. climb trees together, agile, and flexible in relations and in body.

KEY: MAKE FRIENDS.

PURIFICATION — Creative Chaos

Break up the order that you've been conditioned to believe about life. Question everything. Expunge toxic negativity. Unlearn old ways. Create a new story for your life. Reframe your language. think and speak positive. Un-premeditate and un-predict. No analyzing—get out of your mind. Intuit—follow the spontaneous impulse. Know through your body and feelings. Hear voices and have visions. Trust the unconscious. You are not your thoughts. It's crazy wisdom—the genius of the fool.

KEY: THINK DIFFERENT.

KEY: SHOW YOUR COLORS.

RAINBOW — Color

It's a colorful world, so be colorful, expressive, a work of art. Color is energy, so wear all the colors to be the light—integrated, balanced, radiant, the whole spectrum of you. Make magic and materialize a vision and dream. Transform stormy times into rays of hope and success. Follow the rainbow and find your fortune.

REDWOOD TREE — Apotheosis

You have a destiny to fulfill and potentials to realize. It's your apotheosis which you grow into. Keep stretching, extending, and growing yourself like the redwood's reach to be all that you can. Stand up and stand out. Let yourself be pulled and drawn by the life force to your highest expression of self. Head held upwards, aspire to the light. Be the role model, mentor, and standard bearer.

KEY: LIVE LONG.

REEF FISH — Community

Every habitat, including your social circle, workplace, neighborhood, and environment is an ecosystem, a home of variety and commonality. Interact with different others to form an interdependent, integrated community. Accept and weave the web of diversity into a harmonious and functioning system where all benefit in peace and co-evolution. Do your thing and play your part and role. Bring beauty, elegance, art to your world.

KEY: UNIQUE AND UNITED WE SUSTAIN.

RIVER — Flow

Move with the "future pull" on your naturally destined way of self-expression and growth. Let go of control and be taken by your intuitions and impulses. Effortless, no trying, get swept away by the channel of grace in action. In your stream of consciousness, live with the process, always going and becoming. Enjoy the movement, the ups and downs, the bumps and falls, the curves, the thrills, the lulls, the mainstream, and side creeks—the never-ending changes.

KEY: FLOW WITH THE FLOW.

RODENTS — Niche

Find your place, know your function, do your vocation, follow your calling. Be authentic. Work what works for you. Do your right livelihood. In your own niche and suitable position in life, you are special, a specialist known for your unique acuity and particular role. Pay attention to the details, to the minuscule, to the little things that do matter. So natural, so fine, you are unobtrusive.

KEY: RIGHT SIZE YOUR LIFE.

ROOTS — Foundation

Learn the fundamentals. Get your values. Know where you come from, your origins, your strengths and where you want to go. Dig into your place of sustenance and underpinning for the future. Get established, grounded and down to earth. Do the basics—the unglamorous and mundane work to support the heights. Build your infrastructure. Diversify and keep reaching out for what sustains your growth.

KEY: SUCCESS IS AN INSIDE JOB.

SEEDS — Dissemination

You are the future and prospect for coming times. Be responsible to conserve, regenerate and perpetuate. Distribute, disperse, and deliver your gifts, talents, and creativity. Supply, transport and share your energy, wisdom, and skills. Spread and expand the breadth of your influence. Bring life anew. But who knows what, when, where. Be patient and content with being surprised.

KEY: CAST YOUR SEEDS.

KEY: YOU ARE A SENSORIUM.

SENSES — Awareness

Get out of your thinking mind—feel, see, smell, taste, hear. Use your physical senses to be acutely aware and attuned to your surroundings. Taste the truth, see the facts, sound out the way, smell out the situation, feel the vibrations and your sixth sense will intuit the way of extra-sensory perception. Swiftly feel and respond to signals, changes, and influences—sensitive and sensible. And remember to be sensual.

SEX — Orgasm

Maintain physical health and psychological wellbeing by engaging in sexual pleasure and abandonment of self-control. Coupling with another takes you to ecstatic intimacy and bonding. Fulfill your natural instinct and desire for lovemaking, erotic play, and release of tension. Awaken your vital, creative centers and the primordial function of life. Use it or lose it.

KEY: COME ALIVE.

SHEEP — Population

Empathically mirror others and go your way with others. Follow along to get along. Collective intelligence knows what works. Imitate the wisdom of the masses. None of us are as smart as all of us. Large groups are more ecologically efficient, safe, peaceful, powerful, and survivable by their size and numbers than individuals and small groups. Link, connect, gather, share the common. Domesticate, tame your wildness, and curb your individuality. Let go of ego. Be ordinary.

KEY: JOIN THE MAJORITY.

SILICON — Resources

Like silicon, the second most prevalent element in the earth after oxygen, look to the most common and to the nano world for resources. Here, there, and everywhere, your most valuable assets, energy and wealth are right under your feet, in the air, next to you, in your hands and your own DNA. Discover and innovate with your imagination and mimic nature for invention and technology. Small is mighty.

KEY: PUT NATURE TO WORK.

SILVER — Artful

Fashion yourself, work, and life into a conveyor of beauty and utility. You are a medium that conducts utility and luminous aesthetics. Create allure that endures and is valued. Treasured and easy to work with, special and common, apply your art, and shine by design. Let your life reflect your creativity.

KEY: BEAUTY SERVES.

SNAKE — Opportunity

Strike when the open window of opportunity is present. It's the gift of now. Snatch what's hot. Be patient and move with impulse. Coil and be prepared to react with swiftness. Don't hesitate. Trust your instincts and intuitions. Don't show off, just wait and pounce when the chance and time are there. Use the resource of time, it's precious and unrecoverable.

KEY: SEIZE THE MOMENT.

SOIL — Earthy

Your open, welcoming, and generous resources are the indispensable and necessary growing grounds for sustainability. Over time and experience you have become the vital requisite of invaluable sustenance. You may be overlooked and stepped upon but know that you are the stuff and ingredients from which life is made. Unglamorous, do the dirty work from which all others feed. Cultivate your life as if a garden and get down to earth, soiled and fruitful. Seed, produce, harvest.

KEY: THE SOUL GROWS IN SOIL.

KEY: LIFE IS CIRCULATION.

SPIRAL — Cycles

There are no straight lines in the universe, so you will return to where you are now to complete and begin. Move around again and again to hone, develop, refine, and redefine. Renew by recycling. Life is a process, a never-ending journey with no finish line. Keep going and revolving to evolve. On the eternal wheel of life, your actions determine your returns. What you give is what you get. It's a circle dance.

STARS — Inspiration

Look to the stars for inspired creation. Cosmic in your celestial origin, turn on your natural radiance. Born of the light, shine your light. Guide, illuminate, reveal, be a way shower—seer of the past, sage of the present, and augur of the future. Let wonder and awe transport your imagination to new possibilities and hope.

KEY: BE THE STAR THAT YOU ARE.

STONE — Solidity

Hold up, stay firm, keep it together. Constant, reliable, dependable you are. have structure and maintain it. Rock solid, concentrate, remain focused, set in your ways, indivisible, and unwavering in your integrity. Resist fads, infiltrations, and breakdowns. hold and conserve. As the foundation, support and serve the purposes, growth and causes of others. You are the fundament, know these fundamentals of life.

KEY: BE THE ROCK.

SUN — Energy

Within you is a solar energy source that awakens you to consciousness, fuels you with a heated body, fiery spirit and emotional aliveness. Do what gives you energy and energy begets more energy—synergy (sun ergos) results! Be active, but don't burn out. As a sun, spark, catalyze and bring life and warmth to others. Take the lead and be the center. Wear yellow, be bright, sunny, extroverted, passion driven, a fireball of creativity.

KEY: POWERED BY THE SUN!

SUNSET — Reverence

Wherever you are and whatever you are doing, stop in awe of the setting sun. Appreciate in gratitude with the prayer and ritual of "thank you." Your highest respect and sincerest gratefulness ignites and preserves the eternal flame of life within you. Know that all things pass. Welcome change. This spiritual practice inspires you to be the almighty emanation and ray of light that you are. There is no better ally than the divine.

KEY: WORSHIP THE GRANDEUR.

TULIPS — Desire

You are primal and instinctual. Obey your desires. Pursue your seductions. Expose what you want. Mate with life. Show your colors. Reveal your essence. Wear your finest. You are primed and impassioned for magnetizing and receiving. Excited and expectant, full of heated hope, you are the undeniable power of attraction and allure. Under your spell of the sensuous, you evoke craving, longing, and yearning. Your influence inspires and enflames.

KEY: AROUSE!

TURTLE — Longevity

Slowly, slowly, life's a marathon. Take it easy, float along. No hurries and no worries. no clock, take your own time. Trust and relax. Gradually and steadily, step by step, stroke by stroke, results happen. The leisurely way for living long and healthy is to be patient, sure, comfortable, content. Wherever you go, be at home with yourself. You are Turtle Island—mobile home on the voyage.

KEY: GO SLOW.

KEY: LIVE FLUIDLY.

WATER — Sustenance

We live on a water planet and you are water. You need and depend on water—it is your sustainer and absolute imperative resource. Respect, share and cherish it with no wasting. Be water-like — open, flexible, circulating, playful, cleansing, transporting, tempering, flowing, floating, soft. Reflect and be transparent, ever-shifting, and current. Act as a source, oasis, and fountain of life to others.

WAVES — Revolution

Build your life like a wave that is forming larger and fuller. Eventually, you will hit limitation and resistance, so then crash, break up, turn over. Revolution happens. Chaos ensues. Creativity begins. reform and rebuild your next wave. Dance to this never-ending cyclical wave of order into disorder into order. Ride your cycle of waves over and over to prevent your own tsunami. Surf's up! Go for a tumble, live the adventure.

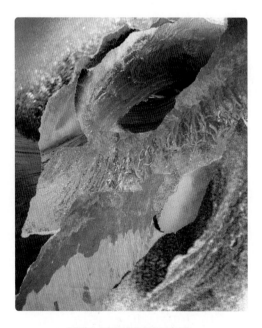

KEY: MAKE WAVES.

WEATHER — Dynamic Equilibrium

You are dynamic—hot and cold, calm and stormy, clear and cloudy—continuously generating energy and inner chi of outer and internal change. Balance, temper and moderate to maintain equilibrium of emotions and expressions that power and influence the conditions of the atmosphere within and around you. Notice and regulate the subtle energies that circulate up and down and all round from the top of your crown to the base of your spine.

KEY: WEATHER THE CHANGES.

WEB — Interconnectedness

You are autonomous, but never alone and isolated. We are all interdependent, related on an ever-connected reciprocal frequency, grid, and matrix of consciousness in continuous synchrony. At once a transmitter and receiver by the web of thoughts, energy vibration and technology, get over the illusion of separation and embrace the oneness.

KEY: INTER-EVERYTHING.

WHALE — Choice

Like whales, originally hoofed land mammals who migrated to the sea, choose the way of life that works for you. Use the pressures of necessity and chance opportunities to create your own niche and position of expression and future. Here you can sing your song. Live loud, large, and long. In your power, gentle and massive, go about your life with no greed, no jealousy, no acrimony. Peace comes from the strength of being happy and true to oneself.

KEY: OPT FOR A WHALE OF A LIFE.

WHEAT — Harvest

Bring in the yield and results of your plan, planting, protection, and production. Reap what you have sown and grown. Now is the time to perform. Prepare and package your output for the payoff. Hold nothing back. It's ripe and ready. No delay and no procrastination. Work, work, work.

KEY: GET IT DONE.

WILD CARD — Surprise

OMG! What is this? Why is this? With a Beginner's Mind, open and wild, take nothing for granted. Expect and anticipate not. Wonder and mystery are the norm. Prediction is fiction. There are more stories than atoms. Sameness and the habitual is death. The unknown is enlivening. Astonish, amaze and surprise—break old roles and routines. Novelty is the way of creation and energy! Mutations happen.

KEY: SEEK MYSTERY.

WILD WOMAN — Expression

Humans have unreasonable emotions, which have intelligence. Let out your feelings and let them guide you. Laugh, cry, erupt, groan, moan, scream. Emotions put you into motion and keep you in motion. Clear and purify by moving cluttered energy out for renewal and direction. Expressiveness is life force in action—vitalizing, animating, enlivening. Get emotionally fit for life.

KEY: EMBODY YOUR FEELINGS.

WINTER — Contraction

Withdraw and Pull Back. Live austerely. Hunker down. Take time out. Be inactive. Go inwards. Invest in yourself to cultivate inner qualities. Hibernate away from activity and busy-ness to conserve and preserve yourself. Detach and find peace. Sleep, meditate, rest. Reflect and refocus.

KEY: RETREAT, RECOVER, RESTORE.

KEY: GROW YOUNG.

YOUTH — Enchantment

Romance your life with the supernatural that allures and enchants. Let go of practical worldly cares and pursue the ecstatic, the magical and mystical. See the beauty and exotic in the everyday mundane. Explore the foreign and taboo as you rebel against the known and boring. believe in your dreams, stories, myths, and superpowers.

About the Author

James Wanless, Ph.D. is an internationally recognized and best-selling author, keynote speaker, futurist and consultant. In his Sustain Yourself Cards, James weaves natural and timeless wisdom with modern-life practicality to guide you along a revolutionary path towards becoming truly self-sustaining personally, professionally, and socially.

This dynamic speaker and educator explores re-energizing mind, heart, body, and spirit for personal and professional balance and growth, the foundations necessary for ultimate social, economic and environ-mental sustainable evolution.

James speaks and trains throughout the world with leaders and companies with the creative right-brain processes in his book, *Intuition@Work*.

James' expertise stems from a deep understanding of holistic, human potential systems, best demonstrated through his best-selling Voyager Tarot Intuition Cards.

For more of James' "green wisdoms" go to: www.sustainyourselfcards.com.